SOUND *Artistry*
INTERMEDIATE METHOD
for TUBA

PETER BOONSHAFT & CHRIS BERNOTAS

in collaboration with
DR. DEANNA SWOBODA

Thank you for making *Sound Artistry Intermediate Method for Tuba* a part of your continued development as a musician. This book will help you progress toward becoming a more able and independent musician, focusing on both your technical and musical abilities. It offers material ranging from intermediate to advanced, making it valuable for musicians at various experience levels.

The many instrument-specific exercises in this book will help to support your personal improvement of techniques on your instrument, focusing on skills that may not always be addressed in an ensemble or in other repertoire. You will notice there are many performance and technique suggestions throughout the book. This wonderful advice has been provided by our renowned collaborative partners, as well as the many specialist teachers we worked with to create this book.

Sound Artistry Intermediate Method for Tuba is organized into lessons that can be followed sequentially. As you progress through each lesson, it is a good idea to go back to previous lessons to reinforce concepts and skills, or just to enjoy performing the music. Exercises include Long Tones, Flexibility, Major and Minor Scales (all forms), Scale Studies, Arpeggio Studies, Chromatic Studies, Etudes, and Duets, as well as exercises that are focused on skills that are particular to your instrument. You will notice that many studies are clearly marked with dynamics, articulations, style, and tempo for you to practice those aspects of performance. Other studies are intentionally left for you to determine those aspects of your musical interpretation and performance. This book progresses through various meters and every key. Once a key has been introduced, previous keys are interspersed throughout for reinforcement and variety. In the back of this book you will also find expanded-range scale pages and a detailed fingering chart.

We wish you all the best as you continue to develop your musicianship, technique, and artistry!

~ Peter Boonshaft and Chris Bernotas

Dr. Deanna Swoboda is an Associate Professor of Music at Arizona State University, where she teaches tuba, euphonium, and music entrepreneurship. As a tuba artist, Dr. Swoboda was the tubist for the internationally recognized Dallas Brass and toured extensively, performing concerts and presenting educational workshops. She is a Past President of the International Tuba Euphonium Association, a recipient of the 2019 ITEA Teaching Award, and an Eastman Music Company Tuba Artist.

alfred.com

ISBN-10: 1-4706-6661-8
ISBN-13: 978-1-4706-6661-3

Instrument photos provided courtesy of Jupiter Band Instruments/KHS America

Lesson 1

DAILY ROUTINE

Start each day with a Long Tone, Flexibility, and Tonguing exercise. This routine will vary from lesson to lesson as new exercises are introduced. Always start your day by trying to achieve your best sound.

1   **LONG TONES**—*When playing long tones, take a full capacity breath and play with a full sound.*

Slowly ♩ = 60

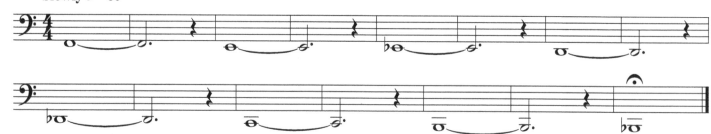

2   **LONG TONES: CHROMATIC**

3   **FLEXIBILITY**

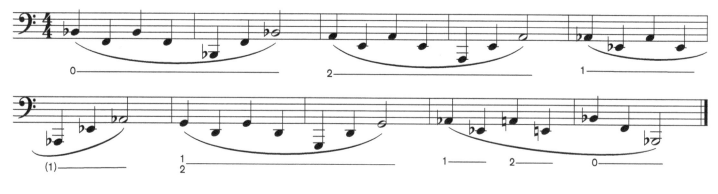

4   **B♭ MAJOR SCALE AND ARPEGGIO**

5   **B♭ MAJOR SCALE STUDY**—*When playing faster scale passages, press the valves firmly and play with even rhythm in the fingers.*

6   **ARPEGGIO STUDY**

7 ETUDE—*Play all etudes slowly with a steady tempo and good tone quality before speeding up. Always keep a good tone in mind and perform with musicality.*

Moderato ♩ = 96

8 ETUDE—*Listen for clarity of articulation in every note.*

Deliberately ♩ = 108

9 ETUDE—*Practice this etude with two-bar phrases and then four-bar phrases.*

Legato ♩ = 80

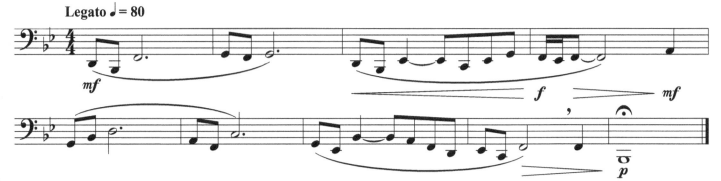

10 DUET   Majestically ♩ = 82

Lesson 2

11 LONG TONES

Slowly ♩ = 60

Play the Flexibility study from Lesson 1 before playing exercise 12.

12 G MINOR SCALE—*For all scale exercises that are written in octaves, practice each octave separately and then as a two octave scale and arpeggio.*

13 G MINOR SCALE STUDY

14 ETUDE

Moderately ♩ = 72

15 ETUDE

Pensively ♩ = 60

16 CHROMATIC SCALE

17 CHROMATIC SCALE ETUDE

Moderately ♩ = 88

18 ETUDE

Lightly ♪ = 120

19 ETUDE—*After playing this etude as written, create or improvise a new ending for the last two measures.*

Moderately ♩ = 100

Lesson 3

20 **LONG TONES**—*Remember to always have proper posture, embouchure, and hand position to promote performing with a beautiful tone.*

Slowly ♩ = 60

21 **FLEXIBILITY**

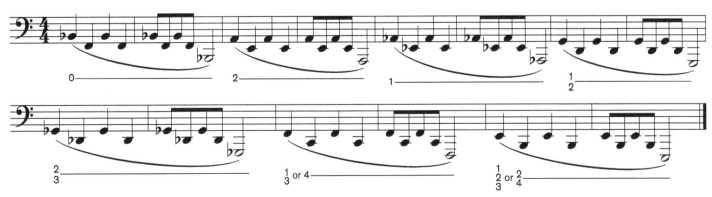

22 **F MAJOR SCALE AND ARPEGGIO**—*Sing or hum these notes before playing them. Internalizing the pitch will help develop your aural skills.*

23 **F MAJOR SCALE STUDY**

24 **ETUDE**

Walking tempo ♩ = 104

25 ARPEGGIO STUDY

26 ETUDE

Allegretto ♩ = 90

27 DUET

Stately ♩ = 88

Lesson 4

Pick a Long Tone, Flexibility, and Tonguing Study/Etude from Lessons 1–3 as your Daily Routine.

28 D MINOR SCALE

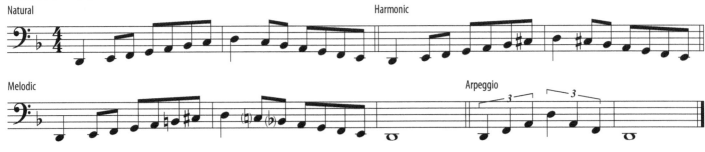

29 D MINOR SCALE STUDY—*Play with firm fingers and smooth air throughout this scale study.*

30 ETUDE

Legato ♩ = 78

mf

31 ETUDE

Moderately ♩ = 88

mf

32 **DUET**—*Work towards matching each of the musical elements in this duet for a unified performance.*

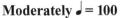

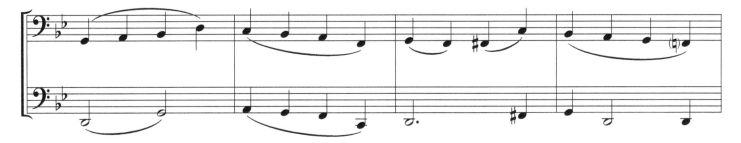

33 **ETUDE**—*Play this etude with an eighth-note pulse until the rhythm is accurate. Then, transition to the dotted-quarter-note pulse.*

Lesson 5

Pick a Long Tone, Flexibility, and Tonguing Study/Etude from Lessons 1–4 as your Daily Routine.

34 **ETUDE**

Allegro ♩ = 120

35 **ETUDE**

Legato ♩ = 88

36 **ETUDE**

Evenly ♩ = 76

37 **ETUDE**

Stately ♩ = 98

38 **DUET**

Maestoso ♩ = 62

39 **ETUDE**

Cantabile ♩ = 72

Lesson 6

Pick a Long Tone study from a previous lesson before playing exercise 40.

40 **FLEXIBILITY**

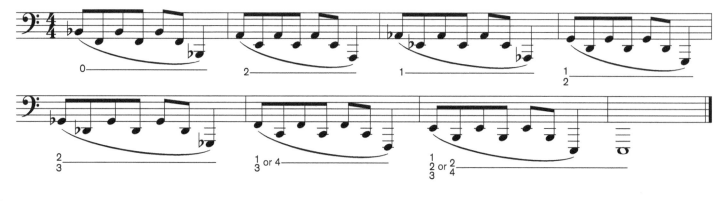

41 **G MAJOR SCALE AND ARPEGGIO**

42 **G MAJOR SCALE STUDY**—*Press the valves firmly and blow with a steady air stream. Using manuscript paper or notation software, compose a new scale study that you think is even more challenging.*

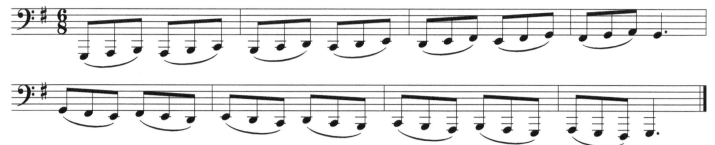

43 **RANGE EXTENSION**

44 **RANGE EXTENSION**

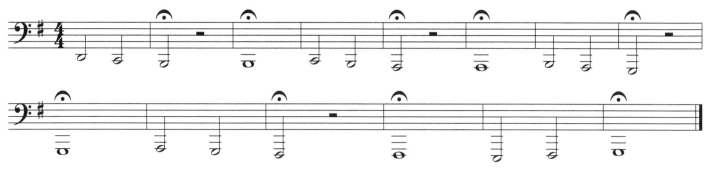

45 **INTERVAL STUDY**—*Once you are comfortable with this as written, practice it an octave higher. Practice this study slurred and then with legato tonguing. Always strive to play with a beautiful sound.*

46 **ETUDE**

Andantino ♩ = 80

47 **ETUDE**—*Practice this etude with two-bar phrases and then four-bar phrases.*

Dolce ♩ = 80

48 **ETUDE**—*Listen for clarity of articulation. Use a "toh" syllable for this style and range.*

Moderately ♩ = 86

Lesson 7

Pick a Long Tone study from a previous lesson before playing exercise 49.

49 FLEXIBILITY

50 E MINOR SCALE

51 E MINOR SCALE STUDY

52 ETUDE

Majestically ♩ = 88

53 COMMON FINGERS

54 ETUDE

55 ETUDE—*After successfully playing this etude, seek guidance from a teacher for ways you can refine your performance.*

56 ETUDE

Lesson 8

Pick a Long Tone study from a previous lesson before playing exercise 57.

57 FLEXIBILITY

58 C MAJOR SCALE AND ARPEGGIO

59 C MAJOR SCALE STUDY

Moderately ♩ = 112

60 ETUDE

Adagio ♪ = 100

61 ETUDE—*Be creative with the musicality of this etude by altering and adding your own dynamic markings.*

Cantabile ♩ = 72

62 DUET

Waltz ♩ = 120

63 A MINOR SCALE

Natural   Harmonic

Melodic   Arpeggio

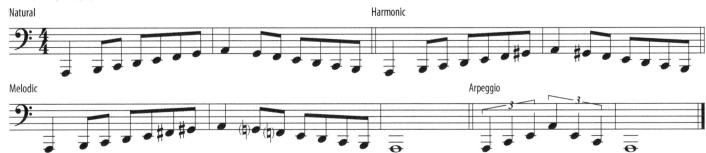

64 A MINOR SCALE STUDY

Moderately ♩ = 80

65 ETUDE

Agitato ♩ = 96

Lesson 9

Pick a Long Tone, Flexibility, and Tonguing Study/Etude from a previous lesson before playing this lesson.

> **GRACE NOTES** are ornaments that are performed before the beat or on the beat, depending on the musical time period, style, context, and notation. The last example below shows how unslashed grace notes would be performed in the Classical period. Listen to music from various historical periods and notice the different approaches to the performance of grace notes.
>
> Most often performed before the beat | Classical period, no slash. On the beat (in time).
>
>

66 **GRACE NOTES**—*Play these grace notes just before the main note.*

Precisely ♩ = 120

67 **ETUDE**

Moderato ♩ = 80

68 **ETUDE**—*An appoggiatura is a grace note without a slash that is played on the beat. In this exercise, measures 1 and 5, as well as measures 3 and 7, would be played the same.*

Cantabile ♩ = 72

69 **ETUDE**

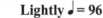 Lightly ♩ = 96

70 **ETUDE**

Andante ♪ = 96

71 ETUDE

Lightly ♩. = 80

Fine

D.C. al Fine

72 ETUDE—*Record your performance of this etude. Recognize the personal musical growth you have made from when you sight-read the piece. Think about the technical and musical ways your performance has improved. Do you hear a difference?*

Pensively ♩ = 72

73 ETUDE—*Play with firm fingers, good air flow, and light articulation.*

Walking tempo ♩ = 82

Lesson 10

74 **LONG TONES**

Slowly ♩ = 60

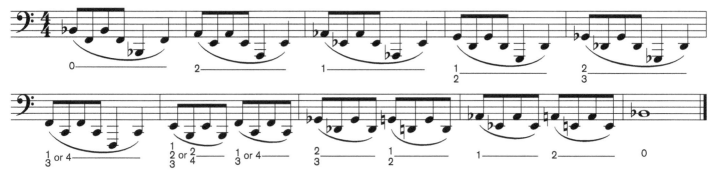

75 **FLEXIBILITY**

76 **ETUDE**

Majestic ♩ = 100

77 **ETUDE**

Pensively ♩ = 60

Page 21

78 CHROMATIC SCALE—Practice this exercise both tongued and slurred. Exaggerate firmly pressing down the valves to keep the rhythm even.

79 CHROMATIC RANGE—Be sure to maintain good air support throughout the exercise. Practice this exercise both slurred and tongued.

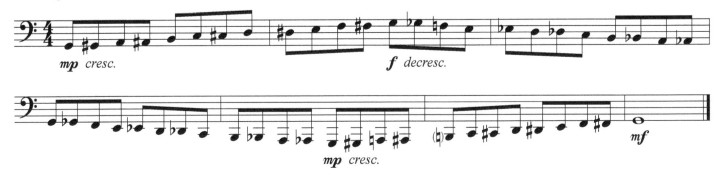

80 MAJOR SCALE RANGE—Keep your body relaxed when playing in the upper register. Practice this exercise both slurred and tongued.

81 DUET

Andante ♩ = 96

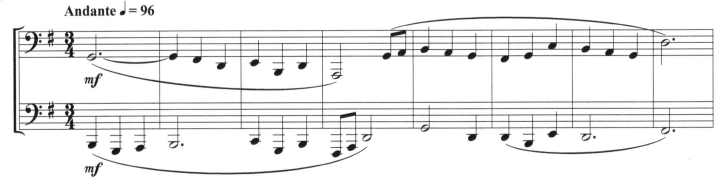

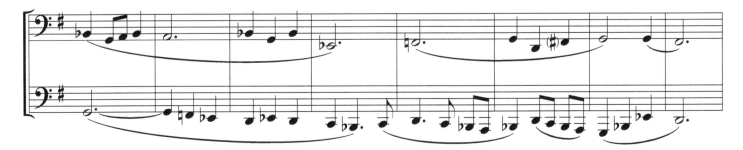

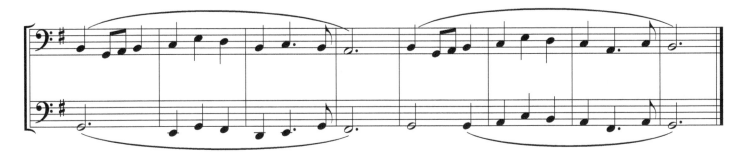

Lesson 11

Pick a Long Tone study from a previous lesson before playing exercise 82.

82 **FLEXIBILITY**—*Remember that constant air support is key for exercises like this.*

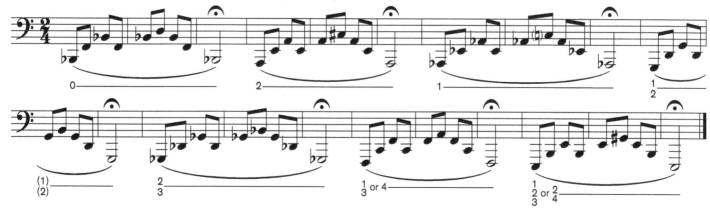

83 **D MAJOR SCALE AND ARPEGGIO**

84 **D MAJOR SCALE STUDY**

Moderately ♩ = 120

85 **ETUDE**

Adagio ♩ = 60

86 **ETUDE**

Andante ♩ = 80

continued on
next page

23

87 ETUDE

88 ETUDE—*After performing this etude, discuss the various elements of the musical work with a peer or teacher.*

89 ETUDE

Lesson 12

Pick a Long Tone study from a previous lesson before playing exercise 90.

90 FLEXIBILITY

91 B MINOR SCALE

Natural   Harmonic

Melodic   Arpeggio

92 B MINOR SCALE STUDY

Strictly ♩ = 100

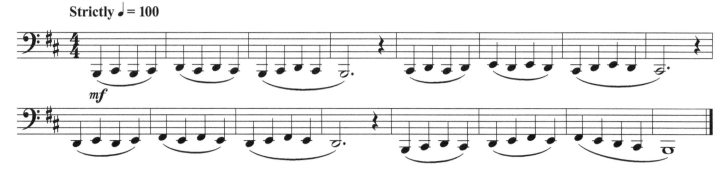

93 B MINOR SCALE STUDY

Moderato ♩ = 112

94 DUET

Andante ♩ = 76   *Fine*

D.C. al Fine

A **TRILL** is an ornament that is performed by alternating rapidly between the written note and the next diatonic note above. Sometimes you will see a natural, sharp, or flat sign with a trill, which means to alternate between the written note and the next altered note. Always check the key signature.

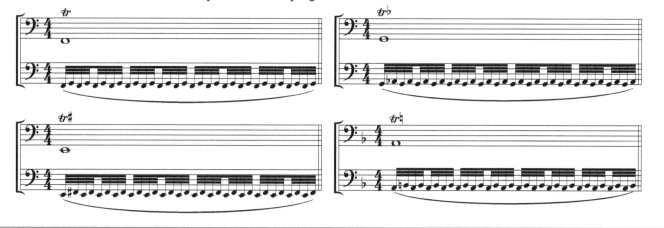

95 **TRILLS**—*Use your metronome to ensure an even and consistent rhythm.*

Evenly ♩ = 72

96 **TRILLS**—*Practice this exercise to ensure your trills are played evenly. Once you are comfortable with this exercise as written, try playing it in cut time (𝅗𝅥=160).*

Presto ♩ = 160

97 **TRILLS**—*Practice measures 1–5 at a slow tempo to reinforce muscle memory, gradually increasing the tempo. This exercise will help ensure that your trills are played evenly.*

Presto ♩ = 144

98 **ETUDE**—*Depending on the style or historical context, a trill may start with an upper neighbor as shown here. Practice these trills with and without the upper neighbor. Also, grace notes are often used at the end of a trill. This ornament is also known as a nachschläge.*

Moderately ♩ = 90

Lesson 13

Pick a Long Tone study from a previous lesson before playing exercise 99.

99 FLEXIBILITY

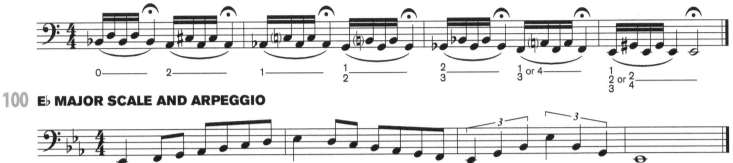

100 E♭ MAJOR SCALE AND ARPEGGIO

101 E♭ MAJOR SCALE STUDY—*Work on your quick breathing in this study. A tuba player must learn to take quick breaths and keep the music flowing, without interrupting the musical line.*

102 ETUDE

103 ETUDE—*For the first phrase of this etude, slur each measure the first time and play staccato the second time.*

104 **DUET**

28

Lesson 14

105 LONG TONES

Slowly ♩ = 60

106 FLEXIBILITY

107 C MINOR SCALE

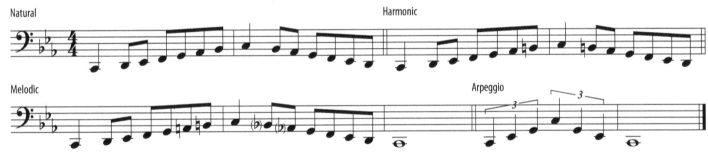

108 C MINOR SCALE STUDY—*Play with firm fingers and a constant air stream.*

Moderately ♩ = 100

109 ETUDE

Larghetto ♩ = 60

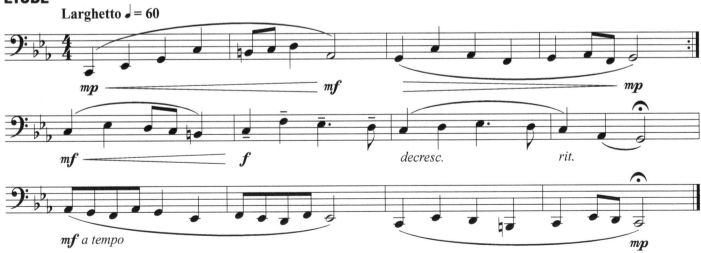

110 **DUET**

111 **ETUDE**

112 **DUET**—*While playing duets, both performers must listen critically to evaluate and adjust intonation.*

Lesson 15

Pick a Long Tone study from a previous lesson before playing exercise 113.

113 FLEXIBILITY

114 A MAJOR SCALE AND ARPEGGIO

115 A MAJOR SCALE STUDY

116 ETUDE

117 ETUDE

118 LONG TONES—*Add a crescendo and decrescendo as you hold each note for at least eight counts.*

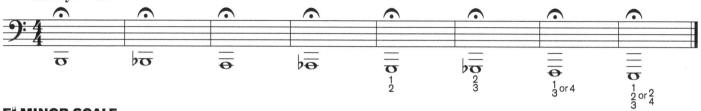

119 F♯ MINOR SCALE

120 F♯ MINOR SCALE STUDY

121 ETUDE

32

Lesson 16

Pick a Long Tone, Flexibility, and Tonguing Study/Etude from previous lessons before playing exercise 122.

122 **DUET**—*When playing ♩♪, remember to think of a sixteenth-note subdivision.*

123 **ETUDE**

124 DUET—*What musical elements in this duet make it engaging? How does the form contribute to the musical work?*

Lightly ♩ = 108

125 ETUDE

Adagio ♩. = 63

Lesson 17

Pick a Long Tone study from a previous lesson before playing exercise 126.

126 FLEXIBILITY

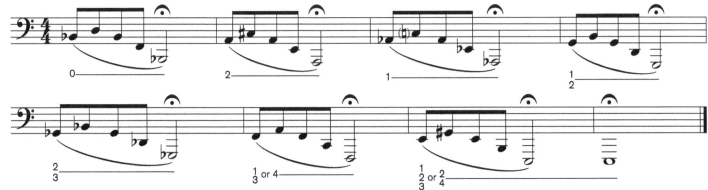

127 A♭ MAJOR SCALE AND ARPEGGIO

A **TURN** or **GRUPPETTO** is an ornament that involves playing the written note, followed by the note above it, returning to the original note, then playing the note below it, and finally ending on the original note.

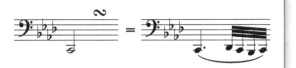

128 A♭ MAJOR SCALE STUDY

Adagio ♩ = 72

129 A♭ MAJOR SCALE STUDY

Moderato ♩ = 112

130 ETUDE

Andante ♩ = 60

continued on next page

131 F MINOR SCALE

Natural   Harmonic

Melodic   Arpeggio

132 F MINOR SCALE STUDY

Allegro ♩ = 132

133 ETUDE

Adagio ♩ = 72

Lesson 18

134 LONG TONES

Slowly ♩ = 60

135 FLEXIBILITY

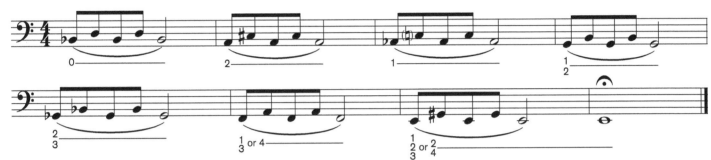

136 E MAJOR SCALE AND ARPEGGIO

137 E MAJOR SCALE STUDY—*Press the valves firmly and evenly in time.*

Andante ♩ = 100

138 ETUDE

Moderate ♩ = 108

139 ETUDE

Adagio ♩. = 60

140 C# MINOR SCALES

141 C# MINOR SCALE STUDY

Moderato ♩ = 108

142 ETUDE

Allegro ♩ = 120

143 DUET

Adagio ♩ = 66

Lesson 19

Pick a Long Tone study from a previous lesson before playing exercise 144.

144 FLEXIBILITY

145 ETUDE

Allegro ♩ = 126

146 ETUDE

Legato ♩ = 72

147 ETUDE

Moderato ♩. = 60

148 **DUET**

149 **ETUDE**

150 **DUET**—*Use critical listening to improve the performance of all musical elements in this duet.*

Lesson 20

Fast, articulated passages often require the use of a technique called **DOUBLE TONGUING**. Double tonguing is a rapid articulation that alternates using the front/tip of the tongue and back of the tongue. Often, the syllables Tu Ku or Du Gu are used to help understand the tongue placement of this technique.

Tu Ku Tu Ku Tu
Du Gu Du Gu Du

151 **DOUBLE TONGUING EXERCISE**—*For this exercise, practice four Tu articulations, then four Ku articulations, working toward making them sound the same. Then, practice double tonguing by alternating between Tu and Ku, still ensuring they sound the same. Use critical listening and experimentation to match the sound of each syllable.*

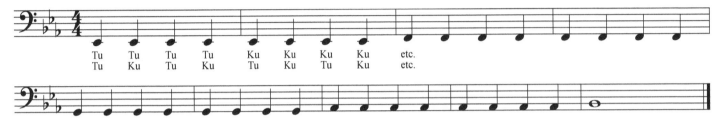

Tu Tu Tu Tu Ku Ku Ku Ku etc.
Tu Ku Tu Ku Tu Ku Tu Ku etc.

152 **DOUBLE TONGUING EXERCISE**—*As you become comfortable with this technique, increase the tempo and perform this exercise in cut time. Apply this pattern to other scales.*

A

Tu Ku Tu Ku Tu etc.

B

Tu Ku Tu Ku Tu Ku Tu Ku Tu etc.

153 **DOUBLE TONGUING EXERCISE**

Fast, articulated passages in three-note groupings often require the use of a technique called **TRIPLE TONGUING**. Triple tonguing is a rapid articulation that alternates using the front/tip of the tongue and back of the tongue. Often, the syllables Tu Tu Ku or Du Du Gu are used to help understand the tongue placement of this technique. Use critical listening and experimentation to match the sound of each syllable.

Tu Tu Ku Tu Tu Ku Tu
Du Du Gu Du Du Gu Du

154 TRIPLE TONGUING EXERCISE

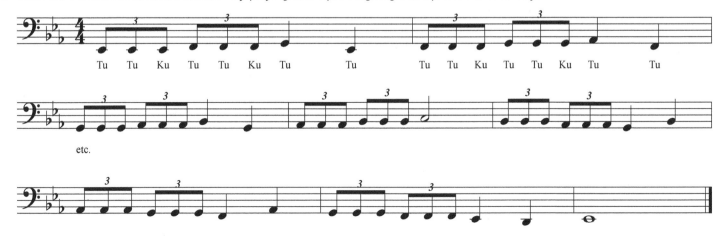

155 TRIPLE TONGUING EXERCISE

156 TRIPLE TONGUING EXERCISE—*Try playing this triple tonguing scale pattern in other keys.*

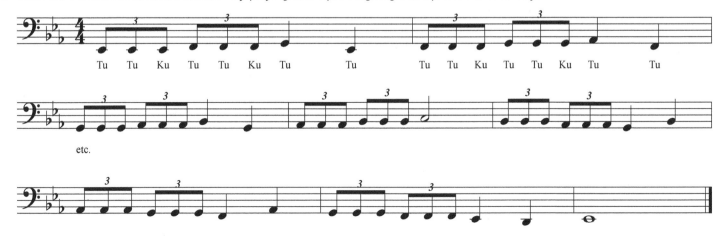

157 **ETUDE (FANFARE)**—*Practice this etude with your fastest and lightest single tongue. Then increase the tempo and change to use double tongue throughout.*

158 **ETUDE (FANFARE)**—*Practice this with both single and triple tonguing.*

159 **DUET**

Lesson 21

Pick a Long Tone study from a previous lesson before playing exercise 160.

Lesson 22

166 LONG TONES

Pick a Flexibility study from a previous lesson before playing exercise 167.

167 B MAJOR SCALE AND ARPEGGIO

168 ETUDE

169 ETUDE

170 A♭ MINOR SCALE *(enharmonic spelling of G♯ minor)*

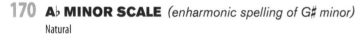

171 ETUDE

Major Scales

C MAJOR

F MAJOR

B♭ MAJOR

E♭ MAJOR

A♭ MAJOR

D♭ MAJOR

G♭ MAJOR

C♭ MAJOR

G MAJOR

D MAJOR

A MAJOR

E MAJOR

B MAJOR

F♯ MAJOR

C♯ MAJOR

Minor Scales

A MINOR

Natural   Harmonic   Melodic

D MINOR

Natural   Harmonic   Melodic

G MINOR

Natural   Harmonic   Melodic

C MINOR

Natural   Harmonic   Melodic

F MINOR

B♭ MINOR

E♭ MINOR

A♭ MINOR

E MINOR

B MINOR

F♯ MINOR

C♯ MINOR

G♯ MINOR

D♯ MINOR

A♯ MINOR

Tuba Fingering Chart

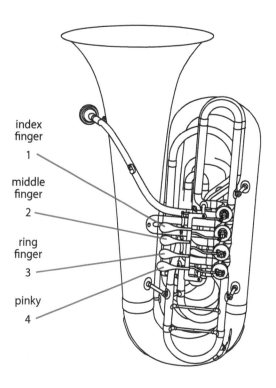

ring finger 3 middle finger 2 index finger 1

index finger 1
middle finger 2
ring finger 3
pinky 4

○ = open
● = pressed down

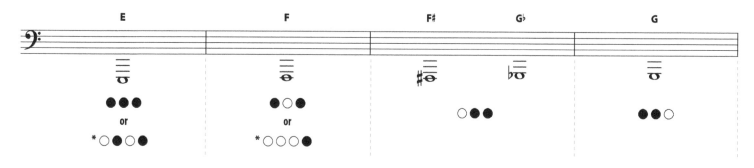

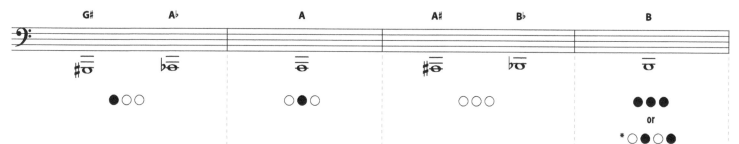

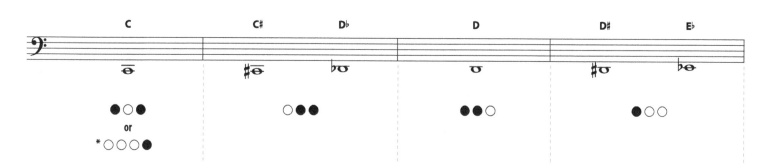

*If playing on an instrument with 4 valves, use the alternate fingering. When using the 4th valve, consider slightly pulling or extending the 4th valve slide.

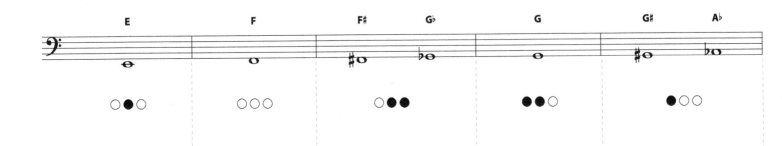

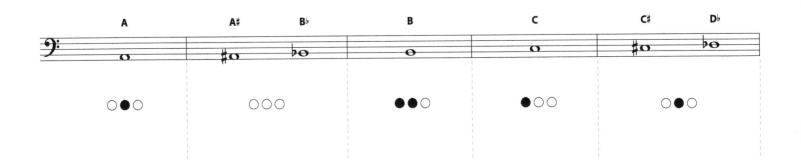

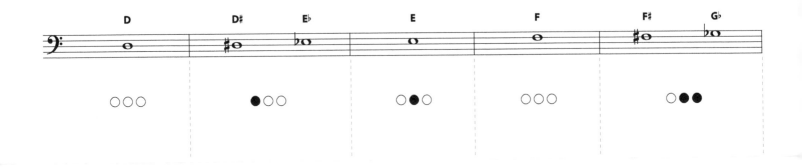

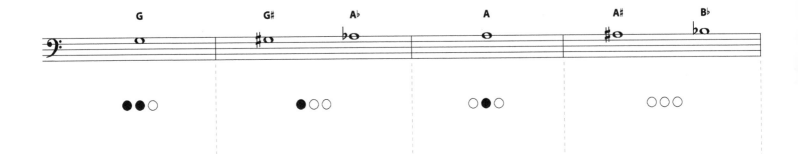